THE WATER ENGINE

&

MR. HAPPINESS

OTHER PLAYS BY DAVID MAMET

AMERICAN BUFFALO
A LIFE IN THE THEATRE
SEXUAL PERVERSITY IN CHICAGO *and* THE DUCK
   VARIATIONS

THE
WATER ENGINE
AN AMERICAN FABLE
AND
MR. HAPPINESS

Two Plays by
David Mamet

GROVE PRESS, INC. / NEW YORK

"The mind of man is less perturbed by a mystery he cannot explain than by an explanation he cannot understand."
—Lenox Lohr, General Manager,
The Century of Progress
Exposition

Both *The Water Engine* and *Mr. Happiness* are set in a radio station studio in 1934. The actors and directors should feel free to use the device of speaking into microphones as much or as little as they wish, and should feel constrained to be consistent only to their own creative fantasies.

In Steven Schachter's productions, in Chicago and New York, many scenes were played on mike, as actors presenting a radio drama, and many scenes were played off mike as in a traditional, realistic play. The result was a third reality, a scenic truth, which dealt with radio not as an electronic convenience, but as an expression of our need to create and to communicate and to explain—much like a chainletter.—D.M.

THE WATER ENGINE
AN AMERICAN FABLE

The Water Engine was first written as a radio play for EAR-PLAY for National Public Radio. The stage version was first produced by the St. Nicholas Theater Company, Chicago, Illinois, May 11, 1977, with the following cast:

CHARLES LANG	W. H. Macy
RITA	Gail Silver
MARTIN KEEGAN (MORTON GROSS)	Michael O'Dwyer
LAWRENCE OBERMAN	Guy Barile
MRS. VAREČ	Belinda Bremner
MR. WALLACE	Norm Tobin
BERNIE	Joseph Weisberg
DAVE MURRAY	Dan Conway

This production was directed by Steven Schachter; set by David Emmons; lighting by Kathleen Daly; original music composed and performed by Alaric Jans.

The New York Shakespeare Festival Public Theater production of *The Water Engine* opened on January 5, 1978, in New York City, with the following cast:

CHARLES LANG	Dwight Schultz
RITA	Penelope Allen
MORTON GROSS	David Sabin
LAWRENCE OBERMAN	Bill Moor
MRS. VAREČ	Barbara Tarbuck
MR. WALLACE	Dominic Chianese
BERNIE	Michael J. Miller
DAVE MURRAY	Colin Stinton

This production was directed by Steven Schachter; set by John Lee Beatty; lighting by Dennis Parichy; original music composed and performed by Alaric Jans; produced by Joseph Papp; associate producer, Bernard Gersten.

The Water Engine opened at the Plymouth Theatre on Broadway on March 6, 1978, New York City, with the following cast:

CHARLES LANG	Dwight Schultz
RITA	Patti LuPone
MORTON GROSS	David Sabin
LAWRENCE OBERMAN	Bill Moor
MRS. VARĔC	Barbara Tarbuck
MR. WALLACE	Dominic Chianese
BERNIE	Michael J. Miller
DAVE MURRAY	Colin Stinton

This production was directed by Steven Schachter; set by John Lee Beatty; lighting by Dennis Parichy; original music composed and performed by Alaric Jans; produced by Joseph Papp; associate producer, Bernard Gersten.

ACT I

Cast members gather at the microphone and sing.

SINGERS: "By the rivers gently flowing,
Illinois, Illinois
Lie thy prairies verdant growing
Illinois, Illinois.
Til upon thine Inland Sea
Stands Chicago, great and free,
Turning all the world to thee,
Illinois, Illinois."

ANNOUNCER (*voice over*): . . . aaand welcome to The Century of Progress Exposition. Yes, the Second Hundred Years of Progress.

Pause.

The concrete poetry of Humankind.
Much is known and much will yet be known.
As we rush on.

Chicago, 1934. The Century of Progress.

LANG *in his laboratory.*

LANG: The techniques of chemistry should not be difficult.
We are all made of chemicals.
We are the world in this respect.

Pause.

Things can work out.
Things can work out if we will persevere.

Pause.

If we will think correctly.
Why must I distinguish between inorganic and organic? All things come from hydrogen. They all come from the earth. As we do. We are made of molecules. We all are made of light. We are the world in this respect.

At the Chicago Daily News. *Newspaper sounds.*

MURRAY: Boy.

BOY: Yessir.

MURRAY: Run this down to the composing room.

BOY: Yessir.

MURRAY: Hold on.

Pause.

I want to ask you something.
"Were it left to me to decide whether we should have a government without newspapers, or newspapers without a government, I should not hesitate to prefer the latter."

Pause.

Do you know who said that?

BOY: No, Mr. Murray.

MURRAY: Good.

SECRETARY: You done?

MURRAY: Yeah. I'm done.

SECRETARY: You want some breakfast?

MURRAY: Yeah.

SECRETARY: Come on.

CHAINLETTER (*voice over*): Neither the Rain nor Snow nor Gloom of Night stays these couriers from the swift completion of their appointed rounds.

At the candystore. Doorbell jingling.

MR. WALLACE: Bernie.

BERNIE: Yeah, Pop.

MR. WALLACE: See who just came in.

MAILMAN: Mailman! Anybody want a letter?

CHAINLETTER (*voice over*): Do not break the chain.

BERNIE: It's only the mailman, Pop.

MR. WALLACE: Hey, Bernie, come here. What did I tell you?

BERNIE: What?

MR. WALLACE: When we close up at night we open up the register.

BERNIE: I'm sorry.

Pause.

MR. WALLACE: Do you know why?

Pause.

BERNIE: Yes, I'm sorry.

At MORTON GROSS' *office.*

SECRETARY (*on phone*): Mr. Gross' office . . . (*Pause.*) No. He's in conference.

CHAINLETTER (*voice over*): Many great and near-great men received this letter. Stanford White received this letter fifteen days before his murder.

Charles H. Lindbergh had received a copy just three days before the kidnapping. Both broke the chain.

SECRETARY (*to recalcitrant inventor in the waiting room*): Sit down, please.

CHAINLETTER (*voice over*): Pass this letter on to three friends. Happiness and health will be yours. One man in Montana received upwards of six thousand dollars. General Burchard in the Philippines received eleven thousand dollars but he lost his life because he broke the chain.

SECRETARY: Sit down, please.

POSTAL PROCESSOR INVENTOR: I want to talk to Mr. Gross about a patent.

LANG *enters office.*

SECRETARY: Yes?

LANG: My name is Lang.

SECRETARY: You have an appointment?

LANG: Yes.

SECRETARY: One minute.

CHAINLETTER *(voice over)* : Do not break the chain.

SECRETARY: You may go in.

LANG: Thank you.

CHAINLETTER *(voice over)* : In September, 1934, a young man in Chicago, Illinois designed—built an engine which used distilled water as its only fuel.

GROSS: Sit down. Sit down.

LANG: Thank you.

GROSS: You are?

LANG: Charles Lang.

GROSS: Glad to meet you.

SECRETARY *(on phone)* : He's in conference.

GROSS: Well, what can I do for you?

LANG: I want to patent something.

GROSS: What?

LANG: An engine.

CHAINLETTER (*voice over*): Write in *your* name at the bottom of the list. Send a postal order for one dollar to the name which appears at the top of the list, and cross that name off the list.

GROSS: Okay, good, tell me about it.

LANG: First we should form an agreement.

GROSS: What?

LANG: First we should form an agreement. If I give you money then we have a contract.

GROSS: You give me a dollar and that's a retainer and that constitutes a contract. Is that what you're saying?

LANG: Yes.

GROSS: Then you can trust me. Is that what you're saying?

LANG: Yes.

GROSS: Fine. Well, then give me a dollar.

Pause. LANG *hands* GROSS *a dollar.*

Thank you. Do you trust me now?

Pause.

And if you couldn't trust me what good would your contract be?

LANG: Well . . .

GROSS: What?

LANG: There is a way things are.

GROSS: All right.

Pause.

Fine. Tell me about your invention.

LANG: Yes, but must we have a contract now?

GROSS (*sighs*) :   Mr. Lang, you're what, you're a designer. I am an attorney, this is what I do, all right? Life is too short. Let's see what we can do for one another here?

LANG: We have a contract?

GROSS: Yes. We have a contract.

Pause.

LANG: I want a patent for my engine.

GROSS: On what basis?

Pause.

What makes it special?

Pause.

LANG: It uses water for its only fuel.

Pause.

It runs on water.

Pause.

GROSS: Who sent you here?

LANG: I saw your name in the telephone directory.

GROSS: No. Who sent you here? Did Jimmy Dwyer at Henrici's send you here?

LANG: I saw your name in the directory.

GROSS: You did.

LANG: It turns out eight horsepower.

SECRETARY (*over intercom*) :   The man with the postal processor is back.

GROSS: Tell him no.

Pause.

Who are you?

LANG: Charles Lang.

GROSS: You show me, Mr. Lang, an engine that can run on water. Show me that. An engine cannot run on water, Mr. Lang.

LANG: I've freed the hydrogen. There's hydrogen in water?

GROSS: Yes.

LANG: My engine runs on it.

GROSS: It does.

LANG: Yes. You can see it.

GROSS: I can.

LANG: In my laboratory.

Pause.

GROSS: And you found my name in the phonebook.

LANG: Yes. (*Gives him a paper.*) If you will come this evening you can see it. But I'm . . .

GROSS: What.

LANG: I'm going to go to someone else if you don't come.

GROSS (*smiling*): I thought we had a contract?

LANG: I'll be there this evening.

P. PROC. INVENTOR: I know that he's in there. I can hear him.

LANG (*leaving*): I'll be there this evening.

P. PROC. INVENTOR: You gave me an appointment.

SECRETARY: No, I certainly did not.

P. PROC. INVENTOR: What must I *do*.

LANG *has left.*

GROSS (*over intercom*) :   What have I got on this evening?

SECRETARY: K. of C.

Pause.

GROSS: Cancel it.

P. PROC. INVENTOR: Please. May I go in?

SECRETARY: No, will you go away. Will you please go away?

> P. PROC. INVENTOR *walks to where* LANG *is waiting at the elevator.*

P. PROC. INVENTOR: He won't see me.

LANG: Why?

P. PROC. INVENTOR: He won't see me any more.

LANG: Why?

P. PROC. INVENTOR: He says he's seen me.

ELEVATOR OPERATOR: Down.

P. PROC. INVENTOR (*whispers*) :   I could revolutionize the mails.

ELEVATOR OPERATOR: Down?

P. PROC. INVENTOR: The delivery of mails.

> LANG *gets on elevator.*

LANG: Down. Thank you.

LADY ON ELEVATOR: . . . and Roosevelt had let him in his cell.

LADY 2:   Who told you that?

LADY: My cousin.

LADY 2:   How does she know?

LADY: Well, her brother worked there.

LADY 2:   At the prison?

LADY: No, the paper.

LADY 2 :   And he let him in his cell?

LADY: Yes.

LADY 2 :   Lindbergh?

LADY: Yes. He told her that the Warden said that Lindbergh was allowed to be alone with him until the execution, and whatever he wanted to do with him was fine.

LADY 2 :   No.

LADY: Just as long as he lived.

ELEVATOR OPERATOR :   Five.

LADY 2 :   And so what did he do to him?

LADY: They handcuffed him to the bars.

LADY 2 :   No.

LADY: Yes. And then Lindbergh came in with this *Doctor's* bag . . .

LADY 2 :   No.

LADY: . . . and they put up these curtains, and left him alone with Hauptman.

LADY 2 :   No.

LADY: Until the execution.

LADY 2 :   And he chained him to the bars?

LADY: Yes. And that's why they didn't allow the photographers.

LADY 2 :   You know, I *wondered* about that.

ELEVATOR OPERATOR :   Ground.

LANG :   Where is your telephone?

ELEVATOR OPERATOR *points.* LANG *leaves elevator.*

LADY: And he was hardly breathing when they pulled the switch.

LANG (*on phone in lobby*) :   How are you?

RITA (*on phone*) :   I'm all right.

Pause.

Is he going to come?

LANG :   I think so.

ELEVATOR OPERATOR :   This car up.

RITA :   He wouldn't say?

LANG :   No.

RITA :   Did you tell him, just the way we worked it out?

LANG :   Yes. I think he'll come.

RITA :   You have to watch yourself.

LANG :   I know.

ELEVATOR OPERATOR :   Up.

RITA :   You must watch yourself.

LANG :   I know.

ELEVATOR OPERATOR :   We're going up.

RITA :   You don't. You must be careful. You don't know these people, Charles.

LANG :   I will be careful.

Pause.

I promise.

Pause.

How are you?

RITA :   I am fine.

Pause.

LANG :   Is there anything that I can get you?

1

RITA: No.

Pause.

LANG: I will see you later.

RITA: Yes. You must be careful with these people.

LANG: I will.

She hangs up. Hold. He hangs up.
A knock is heard at RITA's *door.*
The knock is repeated.

RITA: Who is it?

MRS. VARĚC: Mrs. Varěc.

Pause.

RITA: Who?

MRS. VARĚC: Mrs. Varěc. From upstairs.

RITA: Oh yes, Hello.

MRS. VARĚC: I'm going to the store.

Pause.

Can I get you something from the store?

Pause.

RITA: No thank you.

Pause.

Mrs. Varěc, have a nice day.

MRS. VARĚC: And you too.

MR. WALLACE *at his store, behind the counter.* LANG *and* BERNIE *working on a toy airplane.*

MR. WALLACE: You wanna nother cup of coffee?

LANG: No. No thank you, Mr. Wallace.

MR. WALLACE: Do you want a doughnut?

LANG: No.

BERNIE: Why don't we try to hook it to the aileron?

LANG: All right, let's try.

MR. WALLACE: You seen that thing they have over at the Fair the Hall of Science?

LANG: What's that, Mr. Wallace?

MR. WALLACE: The "Rocket Ship."

LANG: No.

BERNIE: Could I please have the pliers?

LANG *hands him pliers.*

BERNIE: Thank you.

MR. WALLACE: Some of the things there, I cannot believe, that they've got in the Future.

BERNIE: They're not only in the Future, Poppa.

MR. WALLACE: No?

BERNIE: Uh-*uh*, they've got 'em *now*.

MR. WALLACE: Yeah. Have you seen that at the Fair there, Mr. Lang? The "Rocket Ship"?

LANG: No.

MR. WALLACE: You should go.

LANG: I went last year.

BERNIE: I think I've got it, Mr. Lang!

MR. WALLACE: It's not as good as last year.

BERNIE: See!

LANG: Bernie, you're absolutely right.

MR. WALLACE: One thing that I like, though. (*Pauses.*) That Hall of Science.

LANG: You've got a good mind for mechanics, Bernie.

MR. WALLACE: "A good mind for mechanics!" He's another Steinmetz!

BERNIE: Thank you, Mr. Lang.

MR. WALLACE: *If* he applies himself.

GROSS *walks into store.*

MR. WALLACE: Yessir?

GROSS: I'm here to meet *him.*

LANG: I'll see you later, Bernie, Mr. Wallace. . . .

MR. WALLACE: Goodnight, Mr. Lang, that's fifteen cents.

LANG *hands him the money.*

MR. WALLACE: Thank you.

BERNIE: Goodnight, Mr. Lang.

LANG: Goodnight, Bernie, you keep working.

GROSS *and* LANG *exit.*

MR. WALLACE: So you fixed your airplane?

BERNIE: Yes.

MR. WALLACE: Good. (*Musing.*) The "Rocket Ship" . . . some of those things in the Future I cannot believe.

BERNIE: They're not just in the Future, Poppa.

MR. WALLACE: No?

BERNIE: Uh-*uh.* They've got 'em *now,* they're right there at the Fair, they've got 'em *now.*

MR. WALLACE: They do?

BERNIE: Yes.

MR. WALLACE: Oh. And what makes you so smart?

(*Pause.*) Let's close up.

GROSS (*outside*):   Well, here we are.

LANG: Yes.

GROSS: Where are we going?

LANG: Not far.

GROSS: You live around here?

LANG: Not far.

GROSS: I looked you up.

LANG: You did?

GROSS: Yes, I know where you live.

LANG: Yes.

GROSS: We aren't going there.

LANG: No.

Pause.

GROSS: Well, that's all right, that's fine.

Pause.

Tell me how many people know. About this thing of yours.

LANG: A friend and I.

Pause.

Me and a friend. You.

GROSS: I checked up on you.

LANG: Yes.

GROSS: I spoke to your company.

Pause.

Dietz.

LANG: How long do you think it will take us to receive a patent?

GROSS: That depends.

LANG: On what?

GROSS: On many things.

Pause.

Do you want to know what they said?

LANG: At my company?

GROSS: Yes.

LANG: No.

Pause.

This is it.

They go into an alley and into LANG's *laboratory.*

GROSS: My god. Who paid for all this?

LANG: Sit down.

GROSS: This is all yours?

LANG: Yes. Sit down.

GROSS: All of this equipment?

LANG: Please don't touch that.

Pause.

This is my engine and this is water.

GROSS: Uh-huh.

LANG: It's distilled. It won't be necessary in the end, but 'til I solve the carburetion it's much cleaner.

LANG *starts to fuel machine.*

GROSS: Yeah. Now can I taste that please?

Does so. LANG *proceeds to fix engine.*

LANG: They told you what I do there.

GROSS: At the factory.

LANG: Yes.

GROSS: Yes.

LANG: Why did you come, then?

GROSS: We have a contract. What's that?

LANG: Just a battery. I use electric charge for the ignition.

GROSS: All right.

LANG: I'm going to start it now.

GROSS: Yeah. Wait. (*Patting pocket.*) You got a cigarette?

LANG: No. What you're going to see is like a sailboat.
My sister says. There are no more factories.
This engine.

Pause.

This engine, Mr. Gross, draws from the Earth. It draws its power from the Earth.

Pause. Preparation.

Now. (*Touches spark. Nothing happens.*)

GROSS: What's the trouble?

Pause.

LANG: Nothing. We um, this is all right. Hold on one second.

Wait. (*Makes a slight adjustment.*)

Pause.

Wait. (*Fiddles.*) All right. (*Touches spark. Nothing happens. Touches spark again. They sit there.*) I can fix this.

GROSS (*getting up*):   Jimmy Dwyer at Henrici's sent you. You tell Jimmy, no, no. I'll tell Jimmy. This is wonderful.

(*Laughing*) "I'm gonna be rich." (*Exiting, laughing*) Who are you, by the way?

Sound. Engine sparks. They stand there.

LANG: There are no more factories.

CHAINLETTER (*voice over*):   . . . and, delayed by the storm she missed the evening mail by seconds.

The woman then ran on after the mail truck, letter in her hand and the postman saw her in the rearview mirror.

Driving home she found her house had been struck down by lightning.

Had she been there just one minute previously she would have perished in the fire.

Remember to enclose a postal order in the sum of One Dollar.

Make the order out in favor of the person whose name appears at the top of the list.

LANG *and* RITA *at the apartment. A radio dance band is heard beneath their conversation.*

RITA: You know what I want?

LANG: No.

RITA: A place with a balcony. We can sit out.

LANG: Yes.

RITA: And feel the breeze.

Pause.

And fans.

Pause.

Electric fans.

LANG: We're going to move from here.

RITA: Where?

LANG: The country.

RITA: Good.

Pause.

We could have a farm.

LANG: Have you been on a farm?

RITA: Yes.

Pause.

When are you meeting with him?

LANG: Tomorrow night.

RITA: Why at night?

Pause.

LANG: He said we must all be careful.

RITA: Yes, we must.

Pause.

Do you trust him?

LANG: No.

RITA: They all are thieves, you know.

LANG: Who?

RITA: All of them are thieves. You moved the engine, didn't you?

LANG: After he left.

RITA: Good.

RADIO ANNOUNCER (*voice over*):   This concludes another evening of "The Music That You Love To Dance To," coming to you from Chicago's Famed Aragon Ballroom on the Great North Side. Until next Wednesday at this time, then, this is Arthur Riddle wishing you Good Night, Good Luck, and very pleasant dreams.

RITA *turns off the radio, silencing the* ANNOUNCER.

CHAINLETTER (*voice over*) : The terror of the Cities of the Night is Stilled Commerce. Demons and the fears of sleep have been eradicated by the watchmen of the modern order. Now we are characters within a dream of industry. Within a dream of toil . . .

LANG *is seen at his factory working his punchpress.*

WORKER : The unit boss come down here.

LANG : He did.

WORKER : Ask the foreman where you were.

LANG : What did he want?

WORKER : He wanted *you.*

Pause.

You know why?

LANG : No.

WORKER : I know why.

LANG : You do.

WORKER : Yeah.

Pause.

You watch yourself.

Whistle blows.

FOREMAN : Lunch!!!

On which note we leave the factory.

A VOICE : If a man worked all his life
And put his life savings into dollars
And he put them in a bag
And someone took it from him
Then where would he be?

Pause.

Had he not worked?
Must he seek charity?

Pause.

The man who took it—When he spent it—Who would
know it was not his?

*In Bughouse Square. There are speakers, passersby, hecklers,
etc.*

SOAPBOX SPEAKER: . . . and every time I feel a thrill of
pride . . .

BUM: You got a smoke, pal, for a Vet?

LANG: I'm sorry. What?

SOAPBOX SPEAKER: When Patriotic Songs are played . . .

BUM: You got a cigarette?

LANG: No.

SOAPBOX SPEAKER: And when Old Glory takes the breeze . . .

LANG: Do you know what time it is?

BUM: No.

LANG (*to another watcher*): Do you know what time it is?

WATCHER: No.

SOAPBOX SPEAKER: I find myself ashamed.

Pause.

Yes. Ashamed. When will we learn to choose between the
quality of our impressions?

Pause.

Simultaneously:

SOAPBOX SPEAKER: Patriot-   BUM: This man is good. I
ism is a real feeling. Yes.   hears the things he's say-

We feel it there beneath our breastbones, in our hearts, our spirits rise. It serves the cause of death.

The SOAPBOX SPEAKER *continues to speak.* LANG *and* MR. GROSS *converse simultaneously.*

GROSS: Lang.

Pause.

Lang.

LANG: Are you late?

GROSS: What?

LANG: Are you late?

GROSS: No.

Pause.

LANG: I was worried.

GROSS: Come on.

LANG: Where?

GROSS: Around the corner.

Pause.

Come on.

SOAPBOX SPEAKER: What is there so attractive in these tearful, pompfilled ceremonies? What is so seductive in them? They support the torture of the ages. The Great War, the pogroms, the Crusades, the Inquisition (may God Bless us all) "My Country Right or Wrong"—in nomine patri, fillii, spiritiis sancti. Let us go and free the Holy Land, The Maine, The Belgian Orphans . . .

ing. I know what he's saying.

WATCHER: Go back to Russia. (*This line should be spoken after the* SOAPBOX SPEAKER *says* ". . . *the pogroms, the Crusades. . . .*")

WATCHER: I was there. Were you?

SOAPBOX SPEAKER: Yes. And if I was not?

Pause.

We support these things, friend, you and I. The power of the torturers comes from the love of Patriotic Songs. We are the Hun.

WATCHER: Go back to Russia.

SOAPBOX SPEAKER: Russia is a fiction, friend. She is a bugaboo invented to distract you from your troubles.

Pause.

There is no Russia. Russia is the bear beneath your bed.

GROSS: How are you?

LANG: I'm fine.

GROSS: Good.

LANG: Where are we going?

GROSS: Not far. Do you ever come here?

LANG: Bughouse Square?

GROSS: Yes.

LANG: No.

GROSS: Well, I do. I like to hear the speeches. Get a different slant on things.

LANG: Where are we going?

Pause.

GROSS: I want you to meet someone.

LANG: Who?

GROSS: A friend.

LANG: Who is he?

GROSS: Someone who is going to help us. Here.

Pause.

OBERMAN: Mr. Lang?

Pause.

Mr. Lang? I'm very glad to meet you.

GROSS: This is Lawrence Oberman.

LANG: Who are you?

GROSS: Charles, I'm going to stop back at my office.

LANG: Who are you? Who is this man?

GROSS: A lawyer. A good friend of mine.

LANG: A patent lawyer?

GROSS: Yes. I'm going back downtown.

LANG: You're leaving.

GROSS: I have things to wrap up, Charles, don't worry.

Pause.

You're in the best of hands.

LANG: You're leaving.

Pause.

GROSS: I swear to you. You're in the best of hands. You take good care of him.

OBERMAN: I will.

GROSS: I'll call you.

OBERMAN: Call me in the morning.

LANG: Wait. No. You must stay with me.

Pause.

GROSS: Charles. (*Softly*) Charles. I want you to stay here and talk to him.

LANG: You stay with me.

GROSS: It isn't necessary.

Pause.

Really. It is not. Now, you come in tomorrow morning. Can you come in around ten?

LANG (*softly*) :   Yes.

GROSS :   What?

LANG :   Yes.

GROSS :   Then you come in then.

> *Pause.*

> (*To* OBERMAN) And you take good care of him.

OBERMAN (*smiles*) : I will.

GROSS :   I know you will. (*To* LANG) I'll see you in the morning.

> *Exits.*

> KNIFE GRINDER *walks through the neighborhood, and is heard softly singing.*

KNIFE GRINDER :   Knives to grind.
I've got your knives to grind.

> *Pause.*

> Knives to grind, I've got your knives to grind.

> *His song is heard and it fades beneath the following dialogue.* LANG *and* OBERMAN *begin to walk.*

OBERMAN :   Well, how are you?

LANG :   Fine.

OBERMAN :   Good.

> *Pause.*

> Do you get up in the Park much?

LANG :   No.

OBERMAN :   Mmm.

LANG :   Not in years.

> *Pause.*

Who are you?

OBERMAN: I am a colleague of Morton's.

LANG: You work with Gross?

OBERMAN: Yes. I have.

LANG: You are a lawyer.

OBERMAN: Yes.

LANG: For who?

Pause.

Who are you a lawyer for?

OBERMAN: Well, Mr. Lang, I hope that I will work for you.

Pause.

LANG: I have a lawyer.

OBERMAN (*smiles*):   Mr. Lang, I represent some interests which are very much concerned with this machine of yours. Now Gross thought, when he perceived the value of your engine, that it would be best for you quite quickly to avail yourself of aid.

Pause.

Specifically, of services which I am equipped to offer.

Pause.

LANG: What does that mean?

OBERMAN: Listen to me: We wish to take your engine and develop and produce and market it in as economic and efficient a manner as possible; and in so doing make great profits for ourselves and you. (*Pauses. Smiles.*) That is what we want.

LANG: You want to license it.

OBERMAN: No, Mr. Lang. We want to patent it. We want to buy it.

LANG (*Pause*):   Oh.

Pause.

OBERMAN: I should get up here more often.

LANG: You want to buy it from me.

OBERMAN: And we want to protect you.

LANG (*Pause*):   Protect me from what?

OBERMAN: Shall we turn back here?

LANG: Protect me from what?

OBERMAN (*sighs*):   You needn't know. Come with us. See your engine made and utilized.

Pause.

Keep control of what you've made.

LANG: I have control. It's mine.

OBERMAN: The law is not precise on some points . . . litigation is expensive.

LANG: If it isn't mine, whose is it?

Pause.

It's mine.

OBERMAN: A substantial case could be made for the ownership of the machine by those who've paid for its development.

LANG: And who is that?

OBERMAN (*Pause*):   Dietz and Federle. The company for which you work. Shall we take one more turn around the block? They could say you had worked on the engine for many months while in their pay and on their premises. Now, you were forced by circumstances—as we know—to do this, and this is unfortunate.

Pause.

Perhaps more so was your . . . your decision to continue work on the machine at your own workshop.

Pause.

The laboratory you have built yourself on Halsted Street is fitted out entirely with tools and material from Dietz and Federle. Then to whom does the engine belong?

LANG: I run a punchpress there. They pay me ninety cents an hour. I never stole a thing from them.

OBERMAN: Now, Mr. Lang, that just is not the truth.

Pause.

Let's not be specious. Everyone has motives, thieves included. They will say you are a thief, and they will be upheld.

LANG: I made the engine.

OBERMAN: Yes. God bless you. Yes. It is a work of genius.

Pause.

Whether you are able to establish ownership is quite another matter.

Pause.

Here we are. (*Smiles.*)

Quite simply, Mr. Lang, my people want the engine. Dietz would deal with us. We'd rather deal with you. But we still deal with whom we must. Will you entertain an offer for the right to patent the machine?

LANG: Then you would own the engine.

OBERMAN: Yes.

LANG: No. I cannot accept that.

OBERMAN: You know, you put us in an unprotected stance here. You do.

32   DAVID MAMET

Pause.

By dealing with you a case could be made for our collusion in the theft.

LANG: What theft?

OBERMAN: Of the machine. I think that in the light of this our offer is—I am not going to tell you that it's generous it may or may not be—but it is eminently reasonable.

Pause.

Can you see that?

LANG: I don't like you.

OBERMAN: Let us not be romantic, Mr. Lang.
Sell us the machine. I swear to you this offer is in your best interests.
Do you think I like conducting business in the park? In darkness?
You're in danger, Mr. Lang. You are.
And those who deal with you are in danger.
I know that you don't believe this, but it's so.
I swear to you.
Sell us the engine.

Pause.

You sleep on what we've talked about.
Call me tomorrow.
Please.

Pause.

OBERMAN *walks off.*

We hear the Bughouse Square SPEAKER.

SPEAKER: Where are the benefits to you and me? That's what I say. Where are the benefits? A couple kids go off to C.C.C., or build a bridge somewhere's, but what about the Wheat? I ask you where's the Wealth, where is the *wealth?*

Now this is what I say.
The ownership of land.
These things do not change.
They don't change with giveaways and murals.
They are Bank Night at the movies.
That's all. That is all I have to say.

Crowd reaction.

MODERATOR: Step down. Thank you. Anybody else would like
to speak? On any subject? Anybody?

At the apartment.

LANG: They said it wasn't mine.

RITA: What wasn't yours?

LANG: The Engine.

RITA: Well, of course it's yours. Whose is it if it isn't yours?

LANG: They said I stole it.

RITA: Who said that?

LANG *gets up to leave.*

Wait, wait, where are you going, Charles, you just came in.

LANG: I have to go back to the Lab.

RITA: No wait. No, Charles, sit down.

LANG: I have to go.

RITA: You sit down and you tell me what went on.

Pause.

Sit down.

Pause.

LANG: They said it wasn't *mine!!!*

RITA: Hush. Hush now.

Pause.

LANG *quiets down.*

Now tell me what went on.

CHAINLETTER (*voice over*):   A Russian Prince, deposed and penniless in Paris sent the letter on, and two weeks later saw an advertisement in the local paper placed there by his long-lost brother whom he thought was dead.
The brother sought some information of the Prince's whereabouts; and he received his just inheritance at last.
An older woman who had been a nurse discovered fifty thousand dollars in a trunk which she had purchased at a railroad auction.
A missionary, deep in China, received a telegram which said his fiancee had died. The last act of his life prior to entering a monastery was to pass the letter on.
Fifteen years later . . .

RAILROAD CONDUCTOR (*announcing a train*):   For Buffalo . . . Rochester . . . Syracuse . . . Albany . . . 125th Street, and Grand Central Station, on Track Five. This is the Twentieth Century Limited. On Track Five.

LANG *storms into* GROSS' *office.*

SECRETARY: One moment, Sir, he's with a client. *Sir* . . .

LANG (*to* GROSS):   Get up.

SECRETARY: I'm sorry, Mr. Gross, he . . .

GROSS: Close the door, please.

SECRETARY *retires.*

What's the matter?

LANG: Get up.

GROSS: Charles, what's the matter?

LANG: You stand up, you punk.

OBERMAN, *who has been at the back of the office, speaks.*

OBERMAN: Mr. *Lang* . . .

LANG: You, too. You people make me sick.

GROSS: Will you sit down, please? Why don't you sit down?

LANG *stands for a moment, he dashes some object to the floor.*

SECRETARY *buzzes.*

Simultaneously:

OBERMAN: Are you in control now?	GROSS (*into intercom*): No, it's nothing.

OBERMAN: Are you all right now?

Pause.

GROSS: Charles, what is it?

OBERMAN: Can you tell us what's happening, Mr. Lang?

LANG: You're funny.

Pause.

GROSS: What is it Charles?

LANG: You didn't know what's in there. You don't know. If you cannot have it, *kill* it.

Pause.

You don't have one idea what you did. There's nothing sacred to you.

OBERMAN: All right. Now, what is it? What?

LANG: You destroyed. You destroyed it.

OBERMAN: What?

LANG: You wrecked my lab.

Pause.

GROSS: Someone wrecked your lab?

LANG: I think that I should kill you.

GROSS: When?

OBERMAN: When was your lab wrecked? (*To* GROSS) See? You
see? I told you.

LANG: I don't know. Last night.

OBERMAN (*to* GROSS):   You see?

LANG: You told him what?

Pause.

OBERMAN: You're in great danger, Mr. Lang.

LANG: You ruined my work.

OBERMAN: "You" . . . who is this "You?" You think that
Gross and I destroyed your lab?

LANG: Yes. You and him.

OBERMAN: We wrecked it. (*To* GROSS) Do you see?

Pause.

Did I tell you?

Simultaneously:

GROSS: Yes.   OBERMAN: Why would we
                                        do that?

LANG: Plans.

OBERMAN: To get your plans.

LANG: Yes.

OBERMAN: They stole your plans.

GROSS: Oh, christ.

Pause.

OBERMAN: Did they steal your plans!!!?

LANG: No.

OBERMAN: No? The plans are safe?

Pause.

Are the plans safe?

LANG: You people are savages.

Pause.

You're animals.

GROSS: Charles, we did not destroy your lab.

LANG: And I came in here to do business with you. We decided to do business.

GROSS: As God is my Witness. Before God, we did not go . . . why would we do a thing like that?

Pause.

Think. *Think* Why???

SECRETARY (*on intercom*):   Are you in?

GROSS: No.

OBERMAN (*interrupting*):   One moment: are the plans safe?

LANG: Why do you play with me? You know if they're safe or not.

Pause.

LANG: If they'd stolen them, you wouldn't let me in, you wouldn't let me in, I'd be arrested somewhere, wouldn't I? For some two-dollar wrench I took from Dietz.

Pause.

OBERMAN: They're safe.

LANG: Yes. They're safe from you.

Pause.

I hid them. You think I'm a fool? I'm not a fool.

Pause.

OBERMAN: They were hidden.

LANG: Yeah. You bet they were.

OBERMAN: In the laboratory.

LANG: No.

OBERMAN: Where?

Pause.

LANG: Somewhere else.

Pause.

Should I tell you where?

OBERMAN: The engine, too?

LANG: The engine, too. Yes.

Pause.

OBERMAN: So they got nothing.

LANG: Oh. Why did you do this, I came to cooperate. I came to do business.

OBERMAN: Who knew?

LANG: You.

OBERMAN: Who else?

LANG: Just you. You two and my sister.

OBERMAN: Would she tell someone? Who might she tell?

Pause.

LANG: Don't you mention her.

Pause.

GROSS: It might just have been a coincidence. Sometimes . . .

LANG: You don't mention her.

OBERMAN: All right. All right. Mr. Lang, you're very lucky. You have no idea . . . *business* communities, who knows, that girl out there at the desk, some cab driver, perhaps . . . there are many ways. I think that we are very lucky here.

Pause.

LANG: We are lucky.

OBERMAN: Yes. Where is the engine?

LANG: Hidden.

OBERMAN: Where?

LANG: Somewhere safe.

OBERMAN: It must remain safe. I am going to have men assigned. Around your lab and with you, personally.

OBERMAN *moves to the intercom to do so.*

LANG: You ruined my lab.

LANG *rises and moves for the door.*

GROSS: Where are you going?

OBERMAN: Lang!

LANG: Just stay out of my way.

OBERMAN: You can't go out there.

LANG: Leave me alone.

OBERMAN: No, you cannot go out there.

LANG: Don't threaten me. Don't threaten me.

Pause.

You are scum. You're nothing.
I'm leaving now, I'm going, maybe I'll come back.
If I come back you're going to meet our terms. Our terms.
And Oberman? I may go up to your company, I may just

say how badly you have botched this up, I make a deal. I go over your head.

Part of the deal, you are gone. The both of you. You come in and you destroy my experiments, my work . . . I say I want *all* of the money and we throw you to the wolves.

Pause.

Get out of my way.

GROSS: Charles . . .

OBERMAN: Wait. Now wait . . .

LANG: You move aside.

OBERMAN: If you walk out that door now we are going to have to go to Dietz and sue you for possession of the plans.

Pause.

You are going to lose.

LANG: You do your worst.

OBERMAN: I'm trying to help you.

LANG: Get out of my way.

OBERMAN: We'll be here until ten this evening. If you find you need our help.

LANG: I don't expect that.

OBERMAN: If you find that you need help.

LANG (*stepping through them*): Excuse me.

LANG *leaves the office.*

OBERMAN: Who said if everyone just acted in his own best interests this would be a paradise on earth.

OBERMAN *buzzes* SECRETARY.

SECRETARY: Yes, Sir.

ELEVATOR OPERATOR: Down? We're going down . . .

CHAINLETTER (*voice over*):   Make sure you send the letter on to someone who you trust will send the letter on. All people are connected.

Pause.

Do not send cash.

ACT II

LANG *is still in the elevator.*

OBERMAN (*voice over*): Who said that if every man just acted in his own best interests, this would be a paradise on Earth?

RITA: They're going to get him now. They're going to get him now.
The whole thing will go down.
It all goes down when we have given up the things we own.

ANNOUNCER (*voice over*): Another chapter, yes, of *Century of Progress!!!*

RITA: We must all be careful.

ANNOUNCER (*voice over*): You'll remember when we last saw the inventor, Charles Lang, he had just left the offices of Morton Gross.

ELEVATOR OPERATOR: Down, we're going down . . .*

WOMAN (*in elevator*): . . . that people . . . just could die of loneliness.

COMPANION: They could?

WOMAN: This doctor said they could. I read it.

COMPANION: Where?

WOMAN: A magazine.

COMPANION: They must have something else.

* The play can be played in one act by proceeding directly from the end of Act I to this line.

WOMAN: What?

COMPANION: A disease.

WOMAN: No, it said people just could die, you know, if they were lonely.

COMPANION: I don't think so.

WOMAN: Well, I read it.

COMPANION: Where?

LANG *is in the lobby of the office building.*

ELEVATOR OPERATOR: Main floor.

COP: Your name Lang?

LANG: What?

COP: Is your name Lang?

Pause.

LANG: Who are you?

SECOND COP: This way, please.

LANG: Wait, who are you?

They start manhandling LANG.

LANG: Wait, who are you? Wait. Wait. These men are taking me. Wait.

COP: One side, please.

LANG: Who are you?

COP: Stand aside, please, folks, Police.

LANG: You're the Police?

Pause.

You're the Police?

SECOND COP: One side, please.

COP: You got him?

LANG: You wait here. You don't do this.

LANG *struggles to get free. A fight ensues.* LANG *breaks free.*

You won't *do* this . . .

COP: Stop him. Halt! Stop that man.

SECOND COP: Stop!

COP: Take the back.

SECOND COP: Stop that man running.

At MR. WALLACE'*s candystore.*

MR. WALLACE: And so then, Bernie, on the train they found this man who had been the designer.

BERNIE: Of the train?

MR. WALLACE: Yes. Of the train.

BERNIE: He built it.

MR. WALLACE: He designed it.

BERNIE: Uh-huh.

MR. WALLACE: So they said, they're late, and no one in the crew could fix the engine.

BERNIE: Yeah.

MR. WALLACE: They tried and tried.

BERNIE: Uh-huh.

MR. WALLACE: And so this man said, "Let me have a look at it," he took a light, and looked all at the engine, and he said, "Give me a hammer."

Pause.

He took the hammer and he found this place, this one place and gave it a little tap, and boom, the engine started right up.

Pause.

Eh? The next week comes a letter for the President of the Railroad, a bill from this man who had fixed the locomotive.

BERNIE: How much?

MR. WALLACE: Well, that's what I'm telling you:

Pause.

Fifteen thousand dollars.

BERNIE: No!

MR. WALLACE: He telephones the man, he says how come you charge me fifteen thousand dollars for one little hammer tap!?

The door opens and LANG *enters.*

BERNIE: Hiya, Mr. Lang.

MR. WALLACE: How *are* you?

LANG: Hello.

MR. WALLACE: We haven't seen you.

Pause.

How you doing?

LANG: Fine.

MR. WALLACE: Good.

Pause.

LANG: Do you have change for a dollar?

MR. WALLACE: Sure. Bernie.

BERNIE: Yes.

MR. WALLACE: Change for a dollar. You been to the fair since we spoke?

LANG: No. I haven't. No. (BERNIE *gives him change.*) Thank you. (LANG *goes to phone.*)

BERNIE: You're welcome.

MR. WALLACE: You working hard?

LANG: Yes.

MR. WALLACE: I know. Yep.

MR. WALLACE (*to* BERNIE):   Close the register.

BERNIE: I'm sorry.

OPERATOR: The Chicago *Daily News*.

LANG: Hello. I'd like to speak to someone.

     Pause.

OPERATOR: Who? I'm sorry . . . ?

LANG: Someone on the . . . (*Pauses.*) City Desk.

OPERATOR: Who?

LANG: I don't care. The Editor.

     Pause.

     I don't care.

OPERATOR: I'm *ringing* . . .

BERNIE: Pop wants to know if you would like some coffee.

LANG: What?

OPERATOR: That line is busy.

LANG: I'll wait. Thank you. What, I'm sorry. What?

BERNIE: You want a cup of coffee?

LANG: No. Thank you.

OPERATOR: I can ring now.

LANG: Thank you.

MURRAY: City desk.

LANG: Yes. Who is this?

MURRAY: This is Dave Murray.

Pause.

What can I do for you?

LANG: You're a reporter?

MURRAY: Yes. What can I do for you?

LANG: I'd like to speak with you.

MURRAY: All right. About what?

Pause.

LANG: My name is Lang.

MURRAY: L-A-N-G?

LANG: I'm an inventor.

MURRAY: Of what?

LANG: I, of *things* . . . of *things*. I'm in some trouble.

MURRAY: What kind?

Pause.

Are you sure that you don't want the science editor?

LANG: Yes. No, please listen to me: I've invented an engine. Some people are stealing my engine.

MURRAY (*Pause*):   Uh-huh.

LANG: No, these people are trying to take my machine.

MURRAY: Are you all right?

SECRETARY *places some galleys in front of* MURRAY. *He reads while he talks with* LANG.

LANG: Please. Oh, please, I swear to you. All the Police are out. They've got them looking for me. Please. I have to talk to you.

MURRAY *covers mouthpiece. Initials paper.*

MURRAY (*to* SECRETARY) :   It's okay. Send it down.

LANG: I have to talk to you.

MURRAY (*into phone*) :   What? Yeah. All right. All right. Come in.

LANG: No. I can't come in.

MURRAY: You say that the cops are after you?

LANG: Yes.

MURRAY: For what?

Long pause.

All right.

LANG: Can you meet me?

MURRAY: Yes.

LANG: Thank you.

MURRAY: Nine o'clock.

LANG: Before that.

MURRAY: Look, I can't. Unless you come in.

Pause.

LANG: The zoo. Can you meet me at the zoo at nine o'clock?

MURRAY: All right.

LANG: The zoo.

Pause.

God bless you.

Pause.

MURRAY: Nine o'clock. Lincoln Park Zoo. (*Sighs.*) Well, a Free Press is the First defense for liberty. Or words to that effect.

LANG *telephones* RITA.

LANG: Rita?

RITA: Yes. Yes. Oh, where are you?

LANG: Are you all right?

RITA: Yes. Please. Charlie, I'm so worried.

LANG: Now, don't worry. Everything is going to be all right. I'm meeting with a man tonight. I'm going to tell the newspapers.

RITA: When?

LANG: This evening.

RITA: Come here now.

LANG: I can't.

RITA: I'm frightened.

LANG: You'll be fine. Just keep the doors and windows locked, and I will come there when I've met with the reporter.

Pause.

RITA: Will you be all right?

LANG: Yes.

RITA: I'm so worried about you, Charlie.

LANG: We will both be fine.

Pause.

I am going to go now, and I'll be there when I've met with him.

RITA: Yes.

LANG: Everything will be all right.

Pause.

RITA: When we are famous.

LANG: Yes.

RITA: And we are safe.

LANG: I have to go now.

Pause.

LANG *hangs up. We hear a knocking at the apartment door.* RITA *does not answer. The knock is repeated.*

RITA *(tentatively)*:   What? Who is it?

MRS. VARĔC: Mrs. Varĕc from Upstairs.

RITA: Oh, good. Oh, thank god.

MRS. VARĔC: Can I get you anything?

RITA: Wait, Mrs. Varĕc . . .

RITA *goes to and unlocks the door.*

MRS. VARĔC: Can I come in?

RITA: Yes. Mrs. Varĕc, come in.

In the candystore.

LANG *hangs up the telephone. The cops are talking to* MR. WALLACE.

COP: Have you seen this man?

MR. WALLACE: Sure.

COP: When?

MR. WALLACE: All the time. He lives around here.

COP: He been in here.

MR. WALLACE: Sure.

COPS: When?

MR. WALLACE: Regularly. He lives in the neighborhood.

COP: He been in today?

MR. WALLACE: No.

Pause.

COP: Thanks.

SECOND COP: Call in.

COP (*to* MR. WALLACE) : Where's your phone?

MR. WALLACE: It's broken.

Cops exit. MR. WALLACE *stays in front of his store watching
cops.*

Stay in the booth there, Mr. Lang. They're right across the
street and they can see you. They're policemen?

LANG: I don't know.

Pause.

MR. WALLACE: Bernie! Bernie.

BERNIE: What, Pop?

MR. WALLACE: Get down here.

BERNIE: I'm coming.

MR. WALLACE: He'll take you out the cellar, out the back.

Pause.

LANG: Thank you.

MR. WALLACE: That's all right.

BERNIE: What, Pop?

MR. WALLACE: You go show Mr. Lang the way out through the
cellar.

BERNIE: What's up?

MR. WALLACE: Just do it.

BERNIE: Sure.

MR. WALLACE: Will you be all right?

LANG: I'm going to see this man.

MR. WALLACE: He'll help you?

LANG: Yes. I'm seeing him tonight, I'll be all right. I only have to wait 'til then.

BERNIE: Are you in trouble, Mr. Lang?

MR. WALLACE (*at window*): My god, they're coming back. (*To* BERNIE) Go!! Go!

BERNIE: C'mon.

They exit.

The cops are circulating. "Have you seen this man?," etc.

At the Hall of Science.

LECTURER: Those men all died a violent death. The railroad tycoon, not five months from that day, was stricken with a rare, wasting disease, and died within the year. The match king took his own life, jumping from a building he, himself, had built. The financier died at the hands of gamblers. All these men, that power, in one Hotel Room that night, here in Chicago.

BARKER: And now we leave the Hall of Science, the hub of our Century of Progress Exposition. Science, yes, the greatest force for Good and Evil we possess. The Concrete Poetry of Humankind. Our thoughts, our dreams, our aspirations rendered into practical and useful forms. Our science is our self.

Pause.

What are our tools, but wishes? Much is known and much will *yet* be known, and much will not be known. Those wishing a re-entry to the Hall at half-price, come and get a ticket. This is our last tour tonight.

Everyone mills toward the door. LANG *lags behind.*

BARKER: Closing up.

Pause.

Closing up.

LANG: I know. Yes. Thank you.

BARKER: You all right?

LANG: What?

BARKER: Are you all right. I've seen you've been here since this afternoon.

Pause.

Are you okay, pal?

LANG: Yes.

BARKER: Sure?

LANG: Yes.

Pause.

BARKER: They're locking up in twenty minutes.

Pause.

Come on, I'll walk you to the gate.

LANG: What?

BARKER: Come on.

Pause.

Come on, we'll take a walk.

Pause.

LANG: Thank you.

BARKER: I'll punch out.

LANG: I have to make a telephone call.

BARKER: You hold on. I'll be right back. I have to punch out.

LANG: What time do you have?

BARKER: Eight-fifteen.

BARKER *exits.* LANG *moves to telephone.* VOICE OVER *is the last of a speech from a different pavilion.*

VOICE OVER: Rocket travel, travel to the stars, the wonder of the Universe at last within our grasp.

Pause.

Men and women walking on the moon within the lifetime of our children. Who knows *what* they will encounter. By the year two thousand. Travel to the moon and planets. Souvenirs available at the Main Gate. The "Rocket" ship, the travel of the Future.

Pause.

The "Rocket" Ship.

LANG (*on phone*): Rita?

MRS. VARĔC: Hello?

Pause.

LANG: Who is this?

MRS. VARĔC: Hello? Who is this?

Pause.

LANG: Charles Lang.

MRS. VARĔC: Charles.

LANG: Who am I talking to. Who is this?

MRS. VARĔC: This is Mrs. Varĕc.

LANG: Mrs. Varĕc.

MRS. VARĔC: From upstairs.

Pause.

LANG: Where is Rita?

MRS. VARĔC: You better come over here.

LANG: Where is she?

MRS. VARĔC: Something went on.

Pause.

LANG: What?

MRS. VARĔC: You better call the cops.

LANG: What happened?

MRS. VARĔC: Call the police and they'll tell you.

LANG: You tell me.

Pause.

You tell me.

MRS. VARĔC (*Pause*) :   They took her.

LANG: They took her.

MRS. VARĔC: Yeah.

Pause.

LANG: Who took her?

MRS. VARĔC: I don't know.

LANG: What happened, for christ's sake?

MRS. VARĔC: They came in here.

LANG: Who?

MRS. VARĔC: I don't know. I told them already.

LANG: What?

MRS. VARĔC: I heard these noises.

LANG: Yes? Yes? What . . .

MRS. VARĔC: I heard this screaming. My husband, we came
downstairs, the door was broke.

Pause.

There was nobody here.

LANG: The police came?

MRS. VARĔC: What?

LANG: Did the police come?

MRS. VARĔC: Yes. They came. They said if you should call to call them up. A special number. Wait. I'm going to give it to you. (*Hunts.*) Hold on: Lakeview 7-3200.

Pause.

You better call them.

Pause.

Or tell me where you are, they said, and they'll come and get you.

LANG: What?

MRS. VARĔC: They'll come and get you.

Pause.

I'm only cleaning up in here.

A long pause. LANG *hangs up.*

MRS. VARĔC: Is that all right?

UNIDENTIFIED VOICE: Yes.

MRS. VARĔC: Will you let me go home now?

VOICE OVER: The Fair is closing. Please proceed to exits on the North and West sides of the Lagoon.

LANG, *again, on the phone.*

SECRETARY: Mr. Gross' office . . .

LANG: Let me talk to Oberman.

SECRETARY: To *who,* sir?

LANG: Let me talk to him.

Pause.

SECRETARY: One moment.

OBERMAN: Hello?

LANG: Where is she?

OBERMAN: Good evening.

LANG: Where is she?

Pause.

OBERMAN: We can help you find her.

LANG: Can you?

OBERMAN: We can find her.

Pause.

LANG: Don't hurt her.

OBERMAN: Do you have the plans?

LANG: I have them.

OBERMAN: Do you have them with you?

Pause.

LANG: I have them.

OBERMAN: Bring them.

LANG: Just don't hurt her.

OBERMAN: Now we understand that you had tentatively scheduled an appointment with a journalist this evening.

LANG (*Pause*) :   I won't.

OBERMAN: You see how that would not be in your own best interests.

LANG: Yes.

Pause.

Let me talk to her.

OBERMAN: One moment.

Pause.

RITA: Hello?

LANG: Rita?

RITA: Charlie!

LANG: Are you all right?

RITA: What?

LANG: Are you *all right?*

RITA: I'm all right, Charlie. Yes. I'm all right.

LANG: I am going to see you in one hour, I'm going to bring the plans, and then we can go home.

RITA: What, *what?* No.

LANG: No, you don't understand. When I give them the plans, they're going to let you go.

Pause.

RITA: No, I don't think that's a good idea.

Pause.

LANG: You don't understand.

Pause.

They are going to hurt you if I do not bring them in.

Sounds. OBERMAN *tries to take the phone.*

RITA: I understand. Yes. Don't you bring them, Charles. They won't make it. They will just destroy it.

OBERMAN *wrenches the phone from* RITA.

LANG: Hello? Hello?

OBERMAN: Where we met last time. In one hour.

Line goes dead. VOICE OVER *is heard through the next dia-logue.*

VOICE OVER: The Fair is closing. Please proceed to exits on the North and West sides of the Lagoon. Lost children can be claimed on the South End of the Architecture Building. The Exhibitors and the Employees of The Century of Progress Exhibition hope that you have had a good day at the Fair, and invite you all to return soon and often.

BARKER: All done?

LANG: What?

BARKER: Are you done?

LANG (*Pause*):   Yes.

BARKER: Come on. I'll walk you to the gate.

They start to walk.

You look glum.

LANG: What?

BARKER: You don't look good.

LANG: No. No.

BARKER: This'll cheer you up. Look what I got in the mail this morning. (*Produces letter and reads*): "The Ancient Mysteries of Egypt and the East are all within the mind of men."

LANG: What is it?

BARKER: It's a chainletter.

VOICE OVER *stops. They stop.* BARKER *reads:*

"Who knows the real power of man's soul?"
"Much good, much pain and misery is caused by our beliefs.
Great Wealth and Fame stand just beyond your grasp.
All civilization stands on trust.
All people are connected.
No one can call back what one man does."

LANG: What?

BARKER: I'm sorry?

LANG: Would you read that part again?

Pause.

BARKER: Sure.

Pause.

"All people are connected."

LANG: Yes, yes.

BARKER: "No one can call back what one man does."

LANG: Yes, that's right.

BARKER (*reading*):   "Much is known and much will *yet* be known and much will not be known."

Pause.

"Write the names of three friends at the bottom of this list. Send one dollar. . . ." Can you beat this, I'm supposed to send a dollar to three people who I've never heard of. . . . Well, here we are.

LANG: Yes.

Pause.

BARKER: Are you all right?

LANG: Yes. I'm all right now.

BARKER: Did I cheer you up a little?

LANG: Yes. You've helped me more that you could know.

Pause.

BARKER: Well, good night.

LANG: Wait. I would like to show you something.

BARKER: What?

LANG (*produces an envelope containing plans*): These are blueprints.

BARKER: Well, you'll have to tell me what they mean.

LANG: It's an engine.

BARKER: Uh-huh.

LANG: And it uses water for its fuel. I made it.

Pause.

I saw it work.

MURRAY *at his desk at the* Daily News.

MURRAY: The quintessence of those things which made our country great. How much more?

SECRETARY (*taking dictation*): They need the two columns.

MURRAY: How much more?

SECRETARY: Two hundred words?

MURRAY: All right.

Pause.

The Century of Progress, sign and symbol of the great essential strength of the Free Market. All around the nations founder and decay . . . the East Turns Red, and senile Europe limps from day to day in search of that lost leader, that forgotten vigor never to return. For Europe is the Old Land, and this is the New. The West is Golden with the promise of prosperity to come. The Principles which made this country made it great, as it *is* great, as, once again, it shall be great. With Trust, with power, with a mutual recognizance . . .

SECRETARY: They'll take it out.

MURRAY: With mutual understanding of the simple grace and the eternal power of "The Bargain Made and Kept To." Here, now, in Chicago, Phoenix of Communities, we, once again, say, "I Will," and rise from the ashes; hardened, strengthened, turned toward the New Day . . . The Day of Progress: The Second Hundred Years of Progress.

SECRETARY: Mmm.

MURRAY: The Century of Progress Exposition enters *its* new life, too, enters on its second year. Let us continue to support it. Thirty.

SECRETARY: Brilliant.

MURRAY: Thank god I don't have to sign it. What have I got on this evening?

SECRETARY: Meeting with that . . .

MURRAY: Right. Right. Mr. Lang. "They stole my engine."

SECRETARY: That's it.

MURRAY: Meet me afterward?

SECRETARY: Maybe.

MURRAY: Eleven.

SECRETARY: Maybe.

MURRAY (*after her*) : I'll call you.

Bughouse Square.

SPEAKER: What happened to this nation? Or did it ever exist? . . . did it exist with its freedoms and slogan . . . the buntings, the gold-headed standards, the songs. With Equality, Liberty . . . In the West they plow under wheat. Where is America? I say it does not exist. And I say that it never existed. It was all but a myth. A great dream of avarice . . . The dream of a Gentleman Farmer.

LANG *at the meeting place with* OBERMAN.

OBERMAN: Where are the plans?

LANG: Where is my sister?

SPEAKER: And I say that we live in the Final Time.

LANG: My sister is not here?

OBERMAN: You come with me.

SPEAKER: With want in the midst of abundance.

LANG: Oh. You'll take me to her.

OBERMAN: Yes.

SPEAKER: As they turn to War in Old Europe, and we live in Fear at Home . . .

LANG: When I give you the plans?

OBERMAN: Yes.

SPEAKER: In the final moments. When we, when America irrevocably ceases to be Europe, and commences the fulfillment of its malevolent destiny as The New World.

OBERMAN: Where are the plans?

LANG: I'm going to tell you. (*Whispers to* OBERMAN.)

MODERATOR: Anybody else who wants to talk? Does anybody want to speak?

Pause.

Anybody want to speak?

OBERMAN: You *what?*

LANG: I put them in the mailbox, Mr. Oberman.

OBERMAN: You *what?*

LANG: You heard me.

OBERMAN: Do you know what you have done?

LANG: Yes.

OBERMAN: Do you know that we are going to *find* them?

LANG: No. You'll never find them.

OBERMAN: Oh, yes. Mr. Lang, we will. For you will tell us where they are. Believe me. You will tell us where they are.

LANG: No. I think you will find that that is not the truth.

MODERATOR: Anybody want to speak? Does anybody want to speak?

At MR. WALLACE's *candystore.*

BERNIE: Some more coffee?

CUSTOMER: Thank you.

BERNIE: So where was I? Oh, yes. So a letter comes . . .

CUSTOMER: Yeah . . .

BERNIE: For the man who owns the railroad.

CUSTOMER: Uh-huh.

BERNIE: It's a bill, for fifteen thousand dollars.

CUSTOMER: No.

BERNIE: Yeah. So he calls the guy up . . .

MR. WALLACE: My boy taking care of you, M'am?

CUSTOMER: Yes, Mr. Wallace.

MR. WALLACE: Good boy. Good.

BERNIE: And so he calls the guy and asks him, "How come fifteen thousand dollars for one hammer tap . . . ?"

CUSTOMER: Yeah.

BERNIE: And so the guy says, "I gave you the hammer tap for nothing, and the fifteen thousand dollars . . ."

CUSTOMER: Yeah.

BERNIE: "The fifteen thousand dollars was for *knowing where to tap.*"

Pause.

Huh?

CUSTOMER: Yeah.

BERNIE: For *knowing where to tap.*

Pause.

CUSTOMER: *Yeah.* Ah *ha . . . !* (*Gets up to leave. Hands* BERNIE *a coin.*)

BERNIE: Thank you.

CUSTOMER: Mr. Wallace . . .

MR. WALLACE: Yeah.

CUSTOMER: You have a good boy here.

MR. WALLACE: I know it. Have a nice day.

CUSTOMER *exits.*

MURRAY *phones in to the* Daily News.

OPERATOR: *Daily News . . .*

MURRAY: Gimme rewrite.

OPERATOR: What?

MURRAY: Rewrite.

OPERATOR: One moment, please.

REWRITE: Rewrite.

MURRAY: Ernie?

REWRITE: Yeah?

MURRAY: Dave Murray.

REWRITE: How are you?

MURRAY: Fine. Ready?

REWRITE: Shoot.

MURRAY: Waukegan, Illinois, David M. Murray, Special to the *Daily News,* today's date, 7:30, make it 6:30 a.m. The mutilated bodies of a man and woman were discovered in the

early morning hours on a stretch of industrial lake frontage
five miles north of Waukegan today, period.
The man and woman both were white and in their early
thirties, period.
The cause of death in both cases appears to have been
drowning, comma, but both bodies bear signs of quite exten-
sive injury, period. The Illinois State Police and the Lake
County Sheriff's Office are conducting a full-scale inquiry,
comma, and an autopsy later in the day should establish
positively the cause or causes of death. Period. That's it.

REWRITE: Got it.

MURRAY: Tell the lab they got a picture they can get off the
State Cops for the late edition.

REWRITE: Right.

MURRAY: It isn't pretty. Can you buzz upstairs?

REWRITE: Sure. (*Buzzes.*)

SECRETARY: City Desk.

MURRAY: How are you?

SECRETARY: Where the hell have you been?

MURRAY: Did you miss me?

SECRETARY: I've been waiting since eleven.

MURRAY: Yeah. I'm sorry, but I just got done.

SECRETARY: Where are you?

MURRAY: In Waukegan.

SECRETARY: I thought that you were going to the zoo, for
god's sake.

MURRAY: Yeah, "they took my engine." Well he stood me up,
I'm up here on these drowning deaths.

SECRETARY: Will you be back today?

MURRAY: I think so. Yeah. I'll call you.

68   DAVID MAMET

SECRETARY: Will you?

MURRAY: Yeah.

SECRETARY: Good.

They hang up.

At the candystore.

MR. WALLACE: Bernie.

BERNIE: What?

MR. WALLACE: What did you do?

Pause.

BERNIE: What?

Pause.

MR. WALLACE: What did you do?

BERNIE: I left the drawer open. (*Pause.*) I'm sorry.

MR. WALLACE: You cannot leave the drawer open in the day.

Pause.

BERNIE: I'm sorry.

MR. WALLACE: Do you want that chemistry set?

BERNIE: Yes.

MR. WALLACE: All right then.

A paperboy drops off a bundle of papers.

PAPERBOY: Papers.

BERNIE *puts the papers up on the counter.*

MR. WALLACE: Thank you. (*Looks at papers.*) Oh, my god.

BERNIE: What?

MR. WALLACE: Oh my god.

BERNIE: What is it, Pop?

MR. WALLACE: I can't believe this.

Pause.

BERNIE: What *is* it?

MR. WALLACE: Sit down. I am going to read you this.

Pause.

"Free day at the Exposition. Monday, Wednesday, Friday afternoons to anybody under twelve when accompanied by an adult."

BERNIE *cheers.*

Do you want to go?

BERNIE: Yes!

MR. WALLACE: Then watch the cash.

MAILMAN: Mailman!

MR. WALLACE: And what have you got for us today?

MAILMAN *hands letters.*

MAILMAN (*to* BERNIE): And it seems I've got one for *you.*

Hands BERNIE *a letter which* BERNIE *opens and reads during the following speech. The letter contains the plans of the Water Engine.*

BARKER: And so we leave the Hall of Science, the Hub of our Century of Progress Exposition. Science, yes, the greatest force for Good and Evil we possess. The concrete Poetry of Humankind.

Pause.

Much is known and much will *yet* be known, and much will not be known. As we complete our second thousand years. In the dilapidated office buildings, and in rooms in Railroad Hotels, in torn and filthy manuscripts misfiled in second-hand bookstores, here rest the vestiges of this and other cultures. Arcane Knowledge in transition from the inaccessible to the occult, as we rush on.

Pause.

Technological and Ethical masterpieces decay into folktales.
Who knows what is true?
All people are connected.

CHAINLETTER (*voice over*):   One man saw the plans for a machine which he was told would run on water as its only fuel. A woman in Tacoma received seven thousand dollars, but she lost her life because she broke the chain.

BERNIE: Hey, Pop.

MR. WALLACE: What?

BERNIE: Look what I got in the mail.

BARKER: The Fair is closing. Those who wish re-entry to the Hall at half-price, see me for a ticket. This is our last tour tonight. They're good tomorrow, though.

MR. HAPPINESS

Mr. Happiness was first produced at the Plymouth Theatre on Broadway on March 6, 1978, New York City, with Charles Kimbrough as MR. HAPPINESS. The production was directed by Steven Schachter; set by John Lee Beatty; lighting by Dennis Parichy; original music composed by Alaric Jans; produced by Joseph Papp; associate producer, Bernard Gersten.

MR. HAPPINESS *is seated at a desk behind an old-fashioned microphone.*

MR. HAPPINESS: One listener writes:
"Dear Mr. Happiness:
I am thirty-five years old, unmarried. I live with my mother. Mr. Happiness, she is a burden on me. I am not unattractive, I've been told, and I've had men friends. I was engaged once in the War, but he died. So I am no stranger to the ways of Love, if you will think back to that period. I am no stranger to wanting and the need of *care.* But, Mr. Happiness, my mother is an invalid who lays around the house; and I have 'done' for her for six years now. Since she left Bill, my brother's in New Haven to come live with me.

The time has come for me to leave. I have been seeing this man who I met at work, and last week he asked me to marry him.

I said 'yes,' please believe me, very quickly. 'What about my mother, though?' I asked.

He said he thought she could come live with us, but I know that he only said that because he thought that's what I would like to hear. *I* do not want my mother living with us.

I am sick and tired of her ways—for lately she has become very grouchy.

Do you think it would be 'alright' if I told her I am moving out and my new husband just won't hear of her coming to live with us so she had better go back to New Haven?

Pause.

"What do you think? As this is almost true.
Also:
How can my marriage after all these years be possibly

considered as unfaithfulness to my late fiancé, who gave his
life that we may live.
Awaiting your reply,
'I've Got some Good Years Left' "

Hmmm.

Dear "I've Got Some Good Years":
    And I'll say you do, and no mistake. Here's what I say:
    Down through the ages it has been a battle inside of the
Race and inside every one of us to balance selflessness and
Greed. And it's still going on.
    Of *course* you have some good years left in you.
    They *all* are good years when they're balanced.

Beat.

The mouth says "take," the hands say "take"—what
does the heart say? *"Give."* That's right. "Give."
    And, Dear, here's where the *Head* comes in. What do
we always say? "Follow the dictates of your Heart, but
Use your Head." And keep your Two Eyes Open. Dear,
it's such sage advice, and it doesn't originate here. I just
echo it.

Pause.

And you know it yourself. Alright.

Pause.

Now your mother. She needs somewhere to go. She is un-
well. She cannot live alone.
    Your brother had her, but six years ago she came to live
with you. We know not why. If he were prone to take her
voluntarily back you wouldn't take the time to write to *me*.
I wouldn't now be *speaking* to you. Fine.
    Your husband says that he would take her in. You find
this unacceptable. Fine. Your Mother. What does she want?
Let's assume she wants to stay right where she is.
    She's old. She is an invalid. Although I *think* you give
us to suspect that she is shamming.

Pause.

If only partially.

We *all* know how infuriating that can be. I'm sure if we could crack the secrets of the unsolved crimes of ages *many, many* would be founded on *exactly* situations like your own.

Alright.

Mom wants to stay, you want her out. Your hubby doesn't *like* the prospect, no. But he's prepared to put her up if you so wish. Your *brother* doesn't want her.

Pause.

I think the *answer* here is "Put her in a Home."

And all you regulars know that I say that seldom.

Seldom.

Have your husband . . . (I think . . . yes.) *approach* your brother on a friendly basis, yes, but not unmindful of the six years you've relieved him of his rightful burden— and *request* that he contribute to her upkeep in the institution.

Now: he may have been sending her money while she lived with *you*. (*Beat.*) We don't *know*. You didn't *tell* us.

Also: in addition to or, if it should *eventuate*, in *place* of monies from your brother, ask your *husband*.

Ask him. What is it we say?

"You never know until you *ask*."

"The worst thing that can happen is they will say 'NO.' "

That is the worst.

You never know until you ask.

Ask hubby to contribute to her maintenance. Between the two of them I'm certain some arrangement can be made to keep her safe, and comfortable, and *cared-for*. In her final years.

Don't be embarrassed. Face the facts. The facts may be *unpleasant*, but they always are the facts.

You *want*, and you deserve to live. (*Beat.*) Live! (*Beat.*) Live.

Think of your warrior fiancé, your fallen fiancé with reverence. Don't forget him, no. He gave his life for you.

But do not *dote* on him. (*Pause.*)
He is dead.
Your sentiments are noble, but they are misplaced.
Keep your respectful memories for him, and give that long lost love to your *new* husband.

Good Luck, and God Bless You,
Mr. Happiness

Alright.
Remember, Friends. (*Beat.*) If it were not *one* thing, it would *surely* be another.
What's important? (*Beat.*) Your *attitude!*
That's Right.
Let's move along.

"Dear Mr. Happiness:
I'm married to a woman who I do not Love."

Beat.

Love. Everyone's talking about Love.
You know, I say it every week, and I'll say it again. The situations that I see—*your* troubles . . . (they're my troubles too) . . .
They had them back in Bible Times (They did. Oh, yes. They did. Just read your Bible), and they'll have them in the future when we . . . *I* don't know . . . we live in *air,* or whatever the Master has in store for us. (*Beat.*)
People do not change.

"Dear Mr. Happiness:
I'm married to a woman who I do not love. I'm forty-one and she is thirty-five. I'm a policeman, and I have four children ranged in age from two to thirteen years. I love them very much. . . ."

There is the story. *There*'s the rub. We do not *act*ually have to read another word. (*Beat.*) *Do* we?

MR. HAPPINESS *sighs. Beat.*

". . . ranged in age from two to thirteen, and I love them very much.

Our home has been a solid one, and no one in our house has ever wanted. (*Beat.*) Or gone without.

Nor will they, come what may. . . ."

Ah. These are Noble Sentiments.

Beat.

". . . come what may. But I have met a woman. Eighteen months ago in the performance of my job, and she and I are deeply in love with each other.

Sighs.

"I want to leave my wife. I know that this will break her and the children's heart.

But I can't live a lie. What can I do?"

And it's signed "Just a Man."

Well, "Just a Man," I'm going to tell you.

Everything is true if you believe it.

You're a *Police* officer. And in your line of work—and may god *Bless* you for it, it's a thankless job—you see a lot of men.

A fellow with a smoking gun is standing over the proprietor of some poor candy store.

"I had to do it. I don't know. I was just *driven* to it.

Beat.

I didn't mean to kill him, but I had to have the money."

Beat.

He *had* to do it, he tells you. He had no choice. The owner's poor wife in the background, what must she think? Her husband's slayer tells her that he "had to do it," and he meant no harm.

But will he stay and stack the shelves, and pay the monthly bills and marshal the accounts?

And will he raise her children? (*Pause.*)
He "had to do it" . . .
Officer, I'm sure that you see *many* things in your job.
During the performance of your duty.
Some young woman hired as a steno fresh from school.
She's working at the bank. *Deeply* in love.
Young and in love.
Her lover yearns for things. A new coat. (*Beat.*)
An evening on the *town* . . . an *auto* . . .
Everybody *else*, it seems, is comfortable. Happy. Free
from want.
The rich live off the poor and live in *luxury*.
They've taken it from *us*. (*Beat.*) Why not take a little
back? A small amount. A hundred dollars.
They will never miss it.
How he reasons with her. "You will not be caught."
"Please. If you love me."
Oh, she loves him, Officer. We know that very well.
But you have caught her with her fingers in the till.
(*Beat.*) She was trusted and she vowed not to betray that
trust. And there she stands, "I had to do it. Please! I could
not *help* myself. I love him. (*Beat.*) I could not *help* my-
self."
But she's broken the *law*.
She's betrayed those to whom she swore allegiance.
And, Officer . . . and I don't care if you don't *ever* like
it . . . *you*'ve taken an oath.
You took (and you may call me "old-fashioned," if you
will. I *am* old-fashioned. I am *proud* of it.)—you took an
oath. To be true to your wife. To care for her and raise
your family.
Not "Sometime."
Not "While it was *comfortable*." No. But *all* the time.
All of the time.
You say you are in love, but how can love thrive on
deceit?
You know that it cannot. You know that only misery
can flourish in deceit.

Do not defile your home.

Do not betray those who love you.

We know how you long. We none of us are strangers to temptation.

But . . . do *not* give in.

You are a man. You have the power to say "no."

Beat.

Say no.

Look your wife and children in the eye, and *build* with them.

Do not defile your home.

Pause.

Please.

Pause.

Mr. Happiness

Confidential to P.G. in Fairfield:

See a doctor. I am neither fit nor qualified to respond to this inquiry.

Beat.

See a doctor.

And, as you know, all correspondence sent to me is *absolutely* confidential.

Absolutely. It is *seen* by no one but myself.

My files are locked and are *available* to no one but myself.

I've told You, Friends, that I've been asked before . . . that I have received *telegrams* and *personal* visits pleading with me to divulge a name. (*Pause.*)

I have received threats.

But let me say it once again and simply: (*Beat.*)

All correspondence sent to me is *absolutely* confidential.

Absolutely.

Pause.

A Young Man writes: "Dear Mr. Happiness:
I am a boy of fifteen, and afflicted with a small, but noticeable misalignment of my spine which causes me to limp. When I was young . . ."

Hmm. I suppose everything's relative . . .

". . . when I was young it was . . ."

What is this?

". . . painful. But through therapy I learned to overcome the pain.
I read a lot, as I cannot play baseball, or dance very well. Although I'm not sure anyone would dance with me if I *could* dance."

MR. HAPPINESS *reads a while to himself, mumbling.*

I'm going to skip the next part here.

Reads to himself.

"The junior *prom* . . ."

Beat.

His problem is how should he ask her to the Junior Prom.

Continues reading.

". . . the *prom* . . . and *advice* that you might give . . . ashamed to speak to my *father* . . ."

Boy. I'm going to stop right here. You *speak* to your father. Your father is *proud* of you. I swear he is.
Do you know why he's proud of you.
Because he *knows* you. Cause he knows how *brave* you are.
And this "Miss X" you mention?
People are not *mind* readers!
It's difficult to *tell* what is in someone else's heart.

The kind of person that someone is.

I'm going to tell you something, son: Miss X?

Now when she looks at you you *think* she shies away.

Well, boy, it's up to you to take the helm.

This woman does not know what's in your heart.

She cannot read your mind!

And when—let's put our cards up on the table here.

Let's not mince words.

When Miss X looks at you she does not see a boy who *limps*, she sees a boy who *wavers*, son. Who vacillates.

People will accept you on the selfsame terms that you accept yourself.

Talk to your father.

I'm sure he is full of pride for you. For your work.

For your reading and achievement.

You have overcome your pain. That was a monumental task.

I know it was. I'm *sure* it was.

The only demon that you have to face right now is *bashfulness.*

And I never met a girl who wasn't charmed by bashfulness.

Charmed. But not won.

Assert yourself. There's nothing deep here. *Ask* her.

Pause.

And have a great time at the Prom.

Yours,

Mr. Happiness *(Beat.)*

P.S.: Drop me a line and tell me if she let you pin her corsage on.

Pause.

Oh. It takes *time.* It all takes *time.*

You know it's been eight years, now. *(Beat.)*

My *golly* how they do go by!

And I'd bet I could count the different problems that

you write me of—and *thank* you, folks, for trusting me. For turning to me with your troubles . . .

I'd bet I could count the different problems that you speak of in, say, thirty thousand letters I've received—*I* don't know. (*Beat.*) It could be twice that number—on the fingers of one hand.

We Need. We Love. We love too much. We love too little . . .

And maybe the most frequent one:

We just do not know who to turn to. (*Beat.*)

We need a friend. (*Beat.*)

Folks, you know that I'm no doctor. I'm no priest.

I'm no professor. Many times I'm *wrong*.

Often I'm wrong.

But in those times when advice I might give—it's only simple common sense—may serve to help you out, you may sit back and say, "My Golly! You know, it all seems so *simple* now. What makes that man so smart?"

Well, folks, I'm going to tell you.

And it's not intelligence. It isn't even insight.

Pause.

It's *distance*.

The ability to see the facts without becoming sidetracked by the *history*.

By—and I know they're painful and they're meaningful —*particulars*. (*Beat.*)

Who said what to whom, and who forgot the birthday.

Yes, it's *distance*, Friends.

And when I tell you that in all the letters that I get the most, the *most* recurrent problem is just this. It boils down to this: We don't know where to *turn*. We feel *alone*. We need a friendly ear to tell our troubles to. . . .

Well, when I say that it sounds hackneyed. It sounds simple. But it's true.

Someone to say, "Why, I did the same thing *myself,* when I was your age." Or "Just wait it out."

Where can we turn? *Where* are our friends?

Who would listen to our woes?

Just look around you. (*Beat.*) Believe me.

Oh. You say, "I couldn't just *presume* on someone!"
(*Beat.*) "I couldn't just *intrude!* What would they *think?!*"
"No. I could never do that."

But just stop and think a second.

Those same folks you say that you could never talk to.

If they came to you and said, "I have a *problem,* and I
wonder if we just could *talk* about it for a moment."

Why, how would you feel? (*Pause.*)

Wouldn't you be glad to help them out?

And you would probably be flattered that they *asked*
you.

Beat.

Now *wouldn't* you?

Beat.

Well then!

Beat.

What makes you think that they'd feel any different if you
asked *them?*

Pause.

We all need a friend, folks, we all need somebody to just
tell our troubles to. (*Beat.*) Somebody with *distance.*

We all need a friend.

Confidential to M.P.D.:

Yes. Absolutely. And no one need ever know.

Don't kid yourself. They'd do the same to you.

Confidential to A.B. in Springfield:

Just read the letter that you wrote to *me* to *him.*

I've sent it back to you and it should be arriving later
in the week.

God bless you.

Takes new letter.

Oh yes. (*Beat.*)
    No. I think that we'll do this one next week. (*Pause.*)
This one can afford to wait a week.

Confidential to "Mistreated":
    I don't want to *hear* about it.
    Take a good *look* at yourself.

Pause.

Friends, I've received quite a number of requests for
"Twenty-Four Hours a Day" from those of you who
couldn't find it in your local bookstores.
    If you'll write to me at:
        Box "K"
        Chelsea Station
        New York, New York, Zone Eleven
and enclose a postal order for Two Dollars, Fifty Cents
. . . that's two dollars for the book and fifty cents for
handling and postage, we will send it out to you.
    Remember to include your name and your return ad-
dress, or else we won't know who to send it *to*.
    God Bless you all. It's a great honor and a privilege to
spend this time with you.

Beat.

And remember:
    If you want to *have* a friend (*beat*) *be* a friend.

    Until next week, then, I remain,

Sincerely yours,

Beat.

Mr. Happiness